Making & Using Flavored Vinegars

Glenn Andrews

CONTENTS

Introduction

Seasoned vinegars are lovely, both to keep for your own use and to give away as special gifts. There are many excellent seasoned vinegars on the market, but yours will be better — fresher, more flavorful, and more unusual. (The price differential is nice, too.)

These vinegars are simple to make. You're limited only by the range of your imagination — and imaginations have a wonderful way of opening up when you begin to stretch them. Start by making some of the versions I'll give you, then create your own, adding whatever herbs, spices, and flavorings sound good to you.

This bulletin is divided into two main sections.

In "Making Flavored Vinegars," you'll find general instructions (heating, steeping, ripening, etc.) for making the vinegars followed by recipes for specific vinegars — Three-Pepper; Thyme, Lemon Peel, and Black Pepper; Raspberry, etc. — and a few hints on making your own wine vinegar from whatever table wine you have left over from time to time.

In the next second section, "Recipes Using Flavored Vinegars," are specifics and suggestions for perking up your cooking in the simplest possible way, by judicious use of your beautiful flavored vinegars. Making these vinegars is fun, but using them is even more fun (and that, of course, is the point of the whole operation!).

Packaging Your Flavored Vinegars

Especially in the vinegars you plan to give away, go for looks as well as flavor. Save attractive bottles (half-pint maple syrup ones, for instance) or check flea markets and yard sales. Make labels from gold press-on notarial seals. Make the bottles pleasing to look at by inserting into them, where appropriate, whole sprigs of herbs, whole (and choice) berries, cinnamon sticks, etc.

One sort of container I've found especially helpful is the 16-ounce reclosable Grolsch beer bottle. (If you live in a state with a bottle bill, you can probably get empties from a friendly liquor store, though drinking the beer is not too difficult a chore for most people.) Grolsch also puts its beer into regular bottles, so be sure to get the ones with the little ceramic swing-away top.

Soak off the labels, then put on your own. (File folder labels work well and come in different colors, or with stripes of color.) My only complaint with these bottles is that I wish they also came in smaller size.

Sterilize your bottles by washing them, then pouring in some boiling water (use a small funnel). Leave the hot water in the bottles for ten minutes, then pour it out and invert the bottles onto paper towels. When they're thoroughly dry, pour in the vinegar, which you've made according to the directions I'll give you. As you will see, some of the vinegars are made right in the bottle by a gradual steeping of ingredients. Others require advance preparation.

If there is any metal on the bottle lid, put a piece of plastic wrap over the opening before capping.

A fine touch when you're giving away your vinegars is to include some recipes for their use as part of the gift. Feel free to borrow a few of my ideas and recipes (for this use only!). Better yet, of course, include a copy of this bulletin.

For wrapping the bottles, I tend to fall back on good old tissue paper in various colors, tied around the neck of the bottle with a satin ribbon. You can also use the brightly colored, shiny-finish bags sold for liquor gift-giving by many gift shops.

Making Flavored Vinegars

Many flavored vinegars can be made right in the bottles in which you will store them or give them away — as long as you have enough time at your disposal to allow for the gradual build-up of flavor by the steeping process. You simply insert the flavoring ingredients into the bottle, add the vinegar — and wait.

If, however, you suddenly decide in mid-December that you want to give your Aunt Minnie some marvelous vinegar for the holidays, you're going to have to speed up the process. To do this, first bruise your seasoning ingredients — smash them as best you can with a garlic press, pepper mill, coffee grinder, or even a hammer. (In the case of fresh herbs, just crumple them up a bit.) Then place them in a jar with a cover (a mayonnaise jar works well), heat the vinegar to the boiling point, and pour it into the jar.

Keep the jar at room temperature, covered. Start tasting the vinegar in a day or two (putting a few drops on a small piece of bread is a good way to do this) so you will know when the flavor is just right. In many cases, the vinegar will be ready in just a few hours.

When you decide to go with the vinegar the way it is, strain out the flavoring ingredients. Now carefully examine the vinegar. If you can see small particles floating around, or if it looks at all cloudy, run it through a coffee filter until it's clear.

Put another small supply of the seasoning ingredients (this time left whole) into the bottles, mostly for looks, and pour in the vinegar.

Other vinegars, such as raspberry, are best made by cooking the main ingredients briefly in the vinegar, then steeping. No matter which method you use, there's very little effort involved and the rewards are tremendous.

All the vinegars will keep indefinitely. If you plan to keep them on hand for a long time, though, it's wise to sterilize the vinegar you use as a base to avoid further development of the cloudy-looking "mother." Because of vinegar's excellent preservative properties, any sprigs of herbs, etc., that you add will stay fresh looking.

The instructions below all make about two cups of vinegar. To make more, just multiply the ingredients.

What Base Vinegars to Use

In each of the sets of instructions below, I've suggested that you use a certain vinegar. There's always a reason for my choices. Red wine vinegar adds to the color of raspberry vinegar; white wine vinegar shows off the Thyme, Lemon Peel, and Black Pepper Vinegar, and so forth. However, please feel free to follow your own inclinations and preferences.

Here are the vinegars you can find in most grocery stores. (You don't need to use the most expensive brands. You'll be making them special enough to please the most epicurean taste.)

Red wine vinegar — Attractive to the eye; mildly gusty.

White wine vinegar — Off-white; delicate in taste.

Champagne vinegar — Not too different from white wine vinegar.

Japanese or Chinese rice vinegar (white or red) — Very subtle, delicate flavor (but be aware that the "seasoned" variety contains sugar).

Distilled white vinegar — Colorless; very acidic; best for such unsubtle uses as Hot, Hot, Hot Vinegar.

Apple cider vinegar — Light brown; strong flavor of apples.

Malt vinegar — Dark brown; very strong but pleasant flavor; can be hard to find except in Canada (where it's used on French fries!)or in England (where it's the preferred condiment for fish and chips).

Sherry vinegar — Brown; strong flavor of sherry; usually imported from Spain; rather expensive.

Of all these possibilities, the best for making most flavored vinegars are the first four — red wine, white wine, champagne, and Japanese rice vinegars. For most purposes, the others have too strong a flavor of their own. (Exceptions: such pungent vinegars as the ones made with hot peppers, shallots, garlic, or onion.)

Making Your Own Base Vinegars

To really start your flavored vinegars from scratch, make the vinegar itself. Some vinegars can't be made at home (Balsamic, for instance, with its many, many years of aging in a succession of barrels made of different woods), but others are well within your capabilities.

Making vinegar is a continuously cycling process — as you use the finished vinegar (which tends to settle to the bottom of the container), you can add more wine, cider, etc. to make more vinegar. Ideally, you should have a small barrel with a spigot toward the bottom and a small hole for filling at the top. I bought one of these, complete with a supply of "mother," the substance that turns wines, cider, etc., into vinegar, from a company called Franjoh Cellars and used it to make some superb vinegar a few years ago. Unfortunately, Franjoh Cellars seems to have disappeared. For that matter, my barrel disappeared, too, in the course of one of my many moves.

After the nice little barrel left my life, I began to notice that certain store-bought vinegars developed the cloudy mother if I kept them around for a month or so after opening. Aha! These were not expensive vinegars. In New England, it was the Pastene brand. When I lived in California, it was Kern. Experiment with inexpensive vinegars. Even a light film on the top of the vinegar indicates the presence of mother.

It takes about two weeks for mother to make vinegar of whatever you decide to add to it. Once you've gotten yourself some mother, you can be plain or fancy with it.

"Fancy" means that you'll use it for just one sort of vinegar — red or white wine, cider, or, if that's the way you live, champagne. To be further fancy, rip up a siphon and use only the vinegar from the bottom of your container.

"Plain" vinegar, which is always my choice, is made from any wine you have left over. (You do have leftover wine from time to time, don't you? If not, use little "splits" of any sort of wine you wish.) To me, this is a very sentimental vinegar. In it went the last few drops of some Dom Perignon champagne we were given, a tablespoon or two of the Chateau d'Yquem we had one magic evening, the remains of the Chateau something-or-other I gave my husband for a birthday one year — and the dregs of innumerable less memorable bottles. All melded together to become a gorgeous

pink vinegar, which I use whenever I want a white wine vinegar —
or a red one!

For "plain" vinegar, you can forget about spigots and filling
holes and oak barrels and just use any container (including the
vinegar bottle in which you find your mother).

In making either plain or fancy vinegar, there's just one thing to
beware of: getting too strong a mix. To avoid this, add just a little
water along with the wine.

RASPBERRY VINEGAR

*Many people consider this the very best of all the flavored vinegars. Because
it's made with fresh fruit, the procedure is a little different from the usual. Don't
omit the sugar or honey; this vinegar needs a touch of sweetening to bring out
its full flavor.*

    2–2½ cups fresh red raspberries, lightly mashed (an equivalent
          amount of frozen raspberries can be used, but if they're
          presweetened, don't add the sugar or honey)
    2   tablespoons sugar or honey
    2   cups red wine vinegar

Combine all the ingredients in the top of a nonaluminum double
boiler. Place over boiling water, turn down the heat, and cook over
barely simmering water, uncovered, for 10 minutes.

Place in a large screwtop jar and store for 3 weeks, then strain to
separate the vinegar from the berries, pressing on the berries to get
out all the juice. If your vinegar is cloudier than you wish, run it
through a coffee filter. Pour into the bottle(s) you plan to use, adding
a few fresh berries.

MAKES ABOUT 2 CUPS.

Shortcut: Paul Corcellet, maker of one of the finest commercial
raspberry vinegars, also markets an excellent raspberry syrup that
you can find in many fancy-food stores. A little of it added to some
red wine vinegar will give you an instant raspberry vinegar, which
may not be quite as tasty as what you can make but is still very
good.

BLUEBERRY VINEGAR

This ultra-chic and ultra-good fruit vinegar is made in exactly the same way as the raspberry vinegar above.

Use your choice of red or white wine vinegar. The red will give a darker color, but it will have a purplish tinge.

An attractive way to bottle this vinegar, after it has been heated, stored, strained, and possibly filtered, is to put some fresh, large blueberries and a small cinnamon stick in each glass jar. The blueberries will stay fresh indefinitely, the cinnamon stick will swell (and add to the flavor of the vinegar), and the look will be extremely appealing.

PEACH, APRICOT, AND OTHER FRUIT VINEGARS

Follow the same system for vinegars made from any fruit, but use white wine vinegar as the base. Can you imagine peach vinegar sprinkled on a fruit salad — or apricot vinegar mixed with mayonnaise and used in a chicken salad? I strongly recommend them.

Peel apricots, peaches, or nectarines before using by dipping them momentarily in boiling water, then removing the skin with your fingers. If they're big, cut the fruits immediately. Continue as you would for Raspberry Vinegar, previous page.

Herbal Vinegars

Your individual taste and the matter of what fresh herbs are available to you will determine what you use in your herbal vinegars.

You can use one herb or a combination of as many as you like. In addition, you can combine herbs with other flavorings.

I'll give you one example each of a one-herb vinegar, a mixed-herb vinegar, and one with other flavors added. In each case, you'll find a few other suggestions. After that, you're on your own.

I prefer white wine or champagne vinegar for all of these, simply because the herbs show up so well in them when you gaze admiringly at the bottles. White rice vinegar gives the same effect, and is pleasantly mild. Distilled white vinegar, to me, is a bit strong-tasting and tends to overpower the herbs.

BASIL AND OTHER SINGLE-HERB VINEGARS

A pattern to follow — you can use any fresh herb. Dill, for instance, is always enjoyed, as is chervil. Tarragon is one of the greatest vinegars of all. Chives make a subtle vinegar — be sure to use a lot of them in the bottles. For small-leaved herbs such as thyme, use an extra sprig or two.

    4   large sprigs fresh basil
    2   cups white wine or champagne vinegar

Put the basil sprigs into a pint bottle and pour in the vinegar (or divide everything between 2 smaller bottles). Seal. Store for 2 to 3 weeks before using. (For quicker, though not easier, herb vinegar, see the instructions on page 4.)

ROSEMARY-TARRAGON VINEGAR
(and Other Herb-Combination Vinegars)

If I had to pick a favorite of the herb vinegars, this would be it. Rosemary and tarragon are a terrific flavor combination, and the sprigs of the two herbs look fascinatingly exotic together.

But there are other good combinations. Any herb goes well with any other herb. You could use several herbs in combination, too. Oregano and dill are interesting together, as are basil and savory.

- 2 large sprigs rosemary
- 2 large sprigs tarragon
- 2 cups white wine or champagne vinegar

Make this just as you would the basil vinegar above. If you're dividing it between two bottles, make sure to put a sprig of rosemary and a sprig of tarragon in each.

THYME, LEMON PEEL, AND BLACK PEPPER VINEGAR
(and Other Combination Vinegars)

Aside from the fact that it's so good-tasting, the appealing look of this vinegar makes it one of the best to give as a present. Other flavoring ingredients to combine with herbs include dill seeds, whole allspice, white peppercorns, cinnamon sticks, orange peel, tiny hot dried red peppers, and celery seed. The mixture known as pickling spice makes an unusual vinegar, too. (Unless you want a hot vinegar, though, be sure to remove the small chili peppers from the pickling spice.)

- 1 large sprig of fresh thyme
- 1 long spiral lemon peel
- 2 heaping teaspoons black peppercorns
- 2 cups white wine vinegar

Put the thyme, lemon peel, and peppercorns into one 1-pint or two 8-ounce bottles. Add the wine vinegar. Seal the bottle. Store for a month before using, giving the bottle a very gentle shake every day or two. (See the instructions on page 4 if you need to make this vinegar for more immediate use.)

Note: If you're using two 8-ounce bottles, use two smaller sprigs of thyme and two smaller spirals of lemon peel. Put one of each plus 1 heaping teaspoon of peppercorns in each of the two bottles.

THREE-PEPPERCORN VINEGAR

The peppercorns involved are black, white, and green. To make a Four-Peppercorn Vinegar, you could add pink peppercorns, though they are the object of a controversy involving possible toxicity, so I don't recommend them.

This is a desperately chic vinegar. It's also very good.

1	teaspoon black peppercorns
1	teaspoon white peppercorns
1	teaspoon green peppercorns, from a jar or can
2	cups white wine vinegar

Bring the vinegar to a boil. Remove from the heat and add the black and white peppercorns. Let sit until cool, then pour into your bottle(s). (If you're using more than one bottle, divide the peppercorns evenly.) Now add the green peppercorns. Store for 2 or 3 weeks before using. There's no need to strain.

HOT, HOT, HOT VINEGAR

Use with caution — though you can vary the fierceness of this vinegar by the number of hot peppers you use. Distilled white vinegar or apple cider vinegar are the ones to use here, because of their strength of flavor.

You will find this handy to have on hand. Not only will you have an instant source of hotness for certain Mexican and Oriental dishes, but you will also always be in possession of fresh hot peppers, since they keep perfectly in the vinegar. You can pull one out, cut off a little of it to use in your cooking, then put the rest of it back into the bottle.

For the very hottest vinegar: Fill a jar with clean, dry hot peppers. Pour in enough vinegar to cover. Seal. Store for a week or two before using. I use a mixture of jalapeños and the smaller, hotter serrano chilis, but you can use any hot fresh peppers you have or are able to find.

For a milder vinegar: Use milder chilis (of course), and smaller amounts of them — or substitute pieces of red or green sweet peppers for part of the chilis. They will add flavor, but not heat.

SPICED JAPANESE RICE VINEGAR

Dieters will be happy to know that this soft, gentle vinegar can be used as a salad dressing all by itself, with no added oil or salt!

1   small, peeled shallot or garlic clove
10 black peppercorns
1   quarter-sized piece of fresh ginger, peeled
2   cups Japanese white or red rice vinegar

Put the shallot or garlic clove, the peppercorns, and the piece of ginger into a bottle. (You may have to cut the piece of ginger in half if the top of the bottle is small.) Add the rice vinegar.

Seal the bottle and store for about 2 weeks before using.

SEVEN-PEPPER VINEGAR

Anything with a name this outrageous is fun to give as a gift, but this also happens to be a very good vinegar. Here's how you arrive at the large number of peppers:

Black peppercorns
White peppercorns
Szechuan peppercorns
Green peppercorns
Sweet green peppers
Sweet red peppers
Hot chili peppers (to make an Eight-Pepper Vinegar,
   you could use red and green hot peppers)
2   cups white wine vinegar

Make this vinegar exactly as you would Three-Peppercorn Vinegar, with these exceptions: Add the Szechuan peppercorns along with the black and white ones, then mince the sweet peppers and chilis very, very finely and add them to the vinegar at the same time as the green peppercorns. This vinegar does not need to be strained; the vinegar will preserve the fresh ingredients. If you're not familiar with Szechuan peppercorns, you'll find them in the Chinese food section of most supermarkets and, of course, in any Oriental market. They add much flavor but no heat.

GARLIC, SHALLOT, OR ONION VINEGAR

Garlic, shallot, or onion vinegar is a good bet for giving a quick shot of pungency to almost anything non-sweet that you're cooking. Shallot vinegar is the mildest of the three and is usually well liked by even those who run screaming at the thought of garlic. Onion vinegar isn't subtle at all, but that's fine. Garlic vinegar — well, garlic lovers think it enhances everything short of chocolate ice cream.

As to what vinegar to use: Garlic and onions seem to demand a vinegar with strength of its own, hence good choices would be apple cider vinegar or white distilled. Shallots, being more delicate, get along well with wine vinegars.

⅓   cup chopped garlic, shallot, or onion
2   cups vinegar (see above for the sorts to use)

Simply combine the chopped garlic, shallot, or onion with the vinegar in a screw-top jar. Store for 2 or 3 weeks, then strain and bottle, inserting the appropriate thing in each bottle — a peeled clove of garlic or shallot or either a piece of onion or a tiny white onion, peeled.

PROVENÇAL VINEGAR

The flavors of Provence in the South of France are glorious. Here's an easy way to add a touch of them to your food.

1   small sprig of thyme
1   small sprig of rosemary
1   small bay leaf
1   large clove garlic, peeled
Orange peel — 1 strip about 1" by 4"
1   pint white wine vinegar

Put the thyme, rosemary, bay leaf, garlic, and orange peel into a 1-pint bottle (or put smaller amounts in each of two 8-ounce bottles). Add the wine vinegar. Seal. Store for a month before using, giving the bottle a very gentle shake every day or two. (If you need this vinegar for more immediate use, follow the instructions on page 4.)

Recipes Using Flavored Vinegars

These crisps are just to get you started using the vinegars you've made. Try these to get the general effect of what can be done, then start inventing your own ways to use them — either by substituting them for the vinegars in other recipes, or by just splashing them in whenever you sense that you'd add a little magic to a dish you're cooking.

If you haven't yet made the vinegar called for in a recipe you want to try, you can substitute others.

HERBED PARTY CHEESE

This is so much better than the herb and garlic and black pepper cheeses you can buy that you'll never go back to them again. You can adjust the amount of garlic up or down to suit your taste (this is a medium amount) and you can multiply the ingredients to make larger batches. The small amount of vinegar makes a big difference to the taste.

6	ounces cream cheese or Neufchatel
½	teaspoon pressed or finely minced garlic
1	teaspoon Tarragon Vinegar (see page 9)
½	teaspoon freshly ground black pepper
4	teaspoons milk
2	tablespoons mixed aromatic fresh herbs (or 2 teaspoons dry herbs plus 4 teaspoons parsley)

Salt to taste (optional)

Combine all the ingredients in a small bowl, mixing well. Serve with freshly made toast squares, Melba toast, or crackers. Makes about ¾ cup. You can use the cheese right away, but it will be even more delicious after being aged for a day or two, covered, in your refrigerator.

ANNA'S MINESTRONE

Even a canned minestrone (or other vegetable soup) is vastly improved by the addition of a small amount of wine vinegar. When it's homemade soup and the wine vinegar has been flavored by you — wow!

It's fun to get a little carried away when making minestrone, throwing in a handful of this and a handful of that. So add any other ingredients you want — potatoes, celery, rice, spinach, or cabbage, for instance.

3	tablespoons olive oil
¾	cup chopped onion
1	teaspoon minced or pressed garlic
2	carrots, sliced
½	green pepper, diced
2	cups cooked kidney beans or garbanzos
2	cups canned ground tomatoes
2	tablespoons fresh basil, torn apart (or use 2 teaspoons dried)
4	cups beef broth or water
½	cup small elbow macaroni or shells
½	cup frozen peas or cut-up green beans (or both)
1	tablespoon Thyme, Lemon Peel, and Peppercorn Vinegar (see page 10)

Salt and freshly ground black pepper to taste

⅓	cup freshly grated Parmesan cheese

Cook the onion and garlic in the oil in a large pot until they're wilted. Add the carrots and green pepper (and any other vegetables you're using) and sauté for 3 or 4 minutes. Add the beans, tomatoes, basil, and broth; bring to a boil; turn down the heat; cover and simmer for 40 minutes. Now add the macaroni and peas and/or beans. Simmer for 10 minutes. Add the vinegar, salt, and pepper. As for the cheese: you can stir it into the soup and call it a cheese minestrone, or you can pass it separately.

SERVES 4 TO 6.

SHISH KEBAB

The vinegar in a marinade for meat or poultry for shish kebab accomplishes two things. First, it tenderizes the meat. Second, it makes it taste wonderful. Who could ask for more?

2   pounds any meat or poultry, cut into shish kebab-size cubes
3   ounces flavored vinegar — any of the herb or combination vinegars, or one with onion or garlic
½   cup salad or olive oil
¼   cup minced onion
1   teaspoon ground coriander (optional)
Salt and pepper to taste

Combine all the ingredients in a bowl and refrigerate for a few hours or overnight, stirring them around occasionally. String the cubes of meat or poultry on metal skewers (or on well-soaked bamboo ones) and grill over charcoal or broil indoors, basting with the marinade and turning the skewers until the meat is brown and done.

SERVES 4 TO 6.

PORK CHOPS DIJON WITH SHALLOT VINEGAR

To me, these are the best pork chops there could ever be.

2   tablespoons butter or margarine
4 ¾-inch-thick pork chops, trimmed of most of their fat
2   tablespoons Shallot Vinegar (see page 13)
1   teaspoon Dijon mustard
½   cup heavy or medium cream
Salt and freshly ground pepper to taste

Melt the butter in a large frying pan over low heat. Add the pork chops and cook, still over low heat, turning occasionally, for about 30 to 35 minutes or until brown and tender. Remove from the pan and keep in a warm place. Now turn up the heat just a little and deglaze the pan by adding the vinegar and stirring well, scraping up any brown bits. Next, stir in first the mustard, then the cream. Simmer, stirring for 2 or 3 minutes, then serve over or under the chops.

SERVES 4.

SZECHUAN CHICKEN SALAD

Spicy but not really hot, this is a marvelous dish. (If you want it hotter, you can add a few drops of Hot, Hot, Hot Vinegar to the pan containing the other flavoring ingredients.) The warm sauce should be poured on at the last minute, but everything can be prepared, ready to go, well in advance. The Szechuan peppercorns and hoisin *sauce are available in most supermarkets.*

4	check breast halves (2 whole breasts)
1	one-inch piece of fresh ginger, peeled
3	large scallions
¼	cup salad oil
2	tablespoons Spiced Japanese Rice Vinegar (see page 12)
1	teaspoon Szechuan peppercorns, finely ground in a coffee mill, peppermill, or mortar and pestle
1	tablespoon *hoisin* sauce
1	tablespoon honey
1	tablespoon tamari or other soy sauce
½	teaspoon pressed or finely minced garlic
¼	cup peanuts or cashews (optional)

Drops of Hot, Hot, Hot Vinegar (optional; see page 11)
Romaine lettuce, shredded

2	medium tomatoes, cut into wedges

Cut a slice the size of a quarter from the ginger and cut one of the scallions into 1-inch pieces. Put these in a fairly large pot with 2 quarts of water. Bring to a boil, then add the chicken breasts, turn down the heat, and simmer for 15 minutes, covered. Remove from the heat and allow to cool for half an hour.

Meanwhile, mince the rest of the ginger and the remaining scallions. Put these in a small pot with the salad oil, the Spiced Japanese Rice Vinegar, the Szechuan peppercorns, *hoisin* sauce, honey, tamari, garlic, and the nuts, if you're using them. Taste the mixture and then, if you want, add just a little Hot, Hot, Hot Vinegar. Set aside for the moment.

When the chicken is cool, remove the skin and bones and tear the meat into shreds. Place in a heat-proof bowl. Make a bed of the shredded romaine on individual plates or one large platter. At serving time, bring the pot with the ginger-oil mixture to a boil, then pour it over the chicken shreds. Mix well, and serve over the shredded romaine. Place the wedges of tomato around the outside of the lettuce.

SERVES 4.

Szechuan Chicken Salad can also be made with leftover chicken. It won't be quite as good, but it will still probably be the best leftover chicken dish you've ever tasted.

CHICKEN BRAISED WITH BASIL VINEGAR

Fabulous dishes of this sort turn up in the cooking of both France and Italy. The flavor of the herb vinegar permeates the chicken and creates a small amount of simple but succulent sauce.

4   tablespoons olive oil
1   three-pound chicken, cut up or quartered
Salt and freshly ground black pepper to taste
¼   cup Basil Vinegar (see page 9)

Rub the chicken with a little salt and pepper. Heat the olive oil in a large frying pan over medium heat, then brown the chicken all over in this. Remove the chicken pieces to a shallow baking dish, pour on the vinegar and bake, uncovered, at 350°F for 35 to 40 minutes, basting 3 or 4 times.

SERVES 4.

CHICKEN WITH BEAUTIFUL BERRIES

To me, this is one of the loveliest dishes in the world — but without the touch of vinegar, it would just be another fairly ordinary way to cook chicken.

You can use chicken breasts, skinned and boned (half a breast per person), but chicken thighs seem more succulent to me. If you use the breasts, your cooking time can be a bit less.

Use either blueberry or raspberry vinegar and any berries available. They don't have to be fresh — frozen blueberries or raspberries (unsweetened) straight from the freezer work well.

2	tablespoons butter
1	tablespoon salad oil
8	chicken thighs (or 4 skinned and boned breast halves)
½	cup minced scallions or shallots
½	cup Raspberry or Blueberry Vinegar (see pages 8–9)
½	cup chicken broth
½	cup heavy cream
½	cup any berries

Heat the butter and oil over medium heat in a large frying pan until the butter starts to foam. Add the chicken and cook for a few minutes, until light brown on both sides. Remove the chicken from the pan, then lower the heat and cook the scallions or shallots in the same butter and oil for about 10 minutes, stirring often.

Now stir in the vinegar, turn the heat up to medium-high, and cook, scraping, until the vinegar has been reduced to about a quarter of its previous volume. Turn the heat back down and add the chicken broth and cream. Simmer, stirring frequently, for 2 or 3 minutes, then put the chicken back in the pan and continue to simmer, stirring and basting, until the chicken is tender and the sauce has thickened a bit — 5 or 6 minutes should do it.

Stir in the berries and cook for just a minute or two more.

SERVES 4.

OVEN BEEF STEW IN RED WINE

This is far from an ordinary, run-of-the-mill beef stew. The wine, vinegar, and herbs transform it. It's easy to make, too, because there's no browning.

1	pound lean stewing beef, in 1-inch cubes
¾	cup finely chopped onion
½	teaspoon minced garlic
½	cup tomato puree
½	bay leaf
¼	teaspoon oregano
2	tablespoons salad oil
2	tablespoons Basil Vinegar (see page 9)
¾	cup red wine
1½	cups peeled and cubed potatoes
½	cup sliced carrots

Combine all the ingredients except the potatoes and carrots in a covered baking dish or Dutch oven. Bring to a boil on top of the stove, then cover and bake at 375°F for 1 hour. Now add the potatoes and carrots and bake, still covered, for another 30 minutes or until everything is tender. Remove the bay leaf before serving.

SERVES 4.

LIVER JULIENNE, VENETIAN STYLE

If you have even a faint liking for liver, you'll be crazy about it when it's cooked this way.

Calves' liver tends to be expensive, but you can use liver from lamb or even pork just as well (if you can find it!).

3	tablespoons olive oil
1	large onion, thinly sliced
1	pound liver (see above), cut into strips about ⅜ inch wide

Salt and freshly ground black pepper to taste

2	tablespoons Garlic, Shallot, or Onion Vinegar (see page 13)
2	tablespoons chopped parsley

Heat the olive oil in a large frying pan over medium heat. Add the sliced onion and cook, stirring often, for a few minutes or until light brown. Remove and reserve the onions, then turn the heat up to moderately high. Add the strips of liver and cook them quickly, tossing, just until they've lost their red look. Sprinkle on a little salt and pepper, put the onions back in the pan, and reheat quickly, tossing. Now add the vinegar and stir everything quickly together. Sprinkle with the parsley.

SERVES 4.

GAZPACHO

Did you ever hear of an uncooked soup containing vinegar and olive oil? Now you have. Gazpacho, the brilliant Spanish soup-salad, is the one, and it reaches perfection when made this way.

¼	cup minced green pepper
¼	cup minced onion
4	large, very ripe tomatoes, peeled, seeded, and chopped (or use Italian canned tomatoes, chopped)
1	large cucumber, peeled and finely chopped
1	cup tomato juice
3	tablespoons olive oil
2	tablespoons Garlic Vinegar (see page 13)

3–4 drops Hot, Hot, Hot Vinegar (see page 11)

Salt and freshly ground black pepper to taste

½	cup croutons (optional)

Combine all the ingredients except the croutons in a large bowl or pitcher. (Or see below for an alternate method.) Chill thoroughly.

Gazpacho often contains bread, so, if you want to follow tradition, add the croutons when you serve the soup.

SERVES 4 TO 6.

The vegetables in Gazpacho are supposed to be finely chopped, not pureed. However, it's possible to make this soup in a food processor if you're careful not to overprocess everything (and it certainly saves a lot of time and work). Use short bursts or "pulses" of power and stop before it all becomes a homogenous mass. And still a third method (it's been said there are as many ways to make Gazpacho as there are Spaniards): Do turn the soup into a semi-puree, but pass little bowls of minced green pepper, onion, tomatoes, cucumbers, and croutons when you serve it.

SEVICHE

Here your flavored vinegar does the cooking, with a little help from lime juice.

1   pound filets of mackerel, salmon, sea bass, or fresh tuna, cut into serving pieces
Salt to taste
½   cup freshly squeezed lime juice
1   tablespoon Garlic Vinegar (see page 13)
¼   cup Spiced Japanese Rice Vinegar (see page 12)
¼   cup minced onion
2   tablespoons salad oil
½   teaspoon (or to taste) Hot, Hot, Hot Vinegar (see page 11)
¼   teaspoon dried oregano
Various garnishes (see below)

Put the fish filets in a mixing bowl and sprinkle with salt. Toss gently. Add the lime juice, vinegars, and onion and toss again. Cover. Refrigerate for at least 6 hours. Add the salad oil and the Hot, Hot, Hot Vinegar. Serve garnished with as many of these as you wish: cubes or slices of avocado; cubes or wedges of tomato; chopped cilantro; minced jalapeño chiles; chopped scallions; chopped hard-boiled eggs.

SERVES 4 AS A MAIN COURSE, MORE AS AN APPETIZER.

BAKED CLAMS OREGANATA

These baked clams make a splendid main course. For an appetizer, just make them in smaller shells.

½   cup minced onion
½   cup minced celery
3   tablespoons olive oil
2   cups of shucked clams, chopped, complete with their juices
    (or 2 6½-ounce cans minced clams, juice and all)
½   cup freshly grated Parmesan cheese
2   slices homemade-type bread, crumbled
1   teaspoon dried oregano
2   tablespoons Oregano or Basil Vinegar (see page 9)
2   slices bacon, cut in half (optional)
Lemon wedges for serving

Cook the onion and celery in the olive oil for a few minutes until limp. Add the clams. Stir over medium heat for 2 or 3 minutes, then add all the other ingredients, except the bacon and the lemon wedges, stirring gently to mix. Put into 4 large scallop shells (these can be found in most kitchenware stores) or ramekins. Top each with a half slice of the bacon, if you're using it. Bake at 425°F for 10 minutes, or until light brown.

Serve with lemon wedges to 4.

CHINESE PASTA SALAD

Always make more of this than you think you could possibly need — people eat a lot of it.

1	pound Chinese egg noodles or spaghetti
5	tablespoons salad oil, divided
2	teaspoons Chinese hot oil (available in the international section of most supermarkets)
2	tablespoons store-bought Chinese sesame oil (don't use the colorless sesame oil available in health food stores and departments; it has an entirely different taste)
2	tablespoons Seven-Pepper Vinegar (see page 12)
3	large scallions, finely minced
4	teaspoons sugar or honey
1	teaspoon salt
¼	cup minced parsley

Boil the noodles or spaghetti until done, following the package instructions. Drain; cool under running water; place in a salad bowl; toss with 1 tablespoon of the salad oil. In a small heat-proof bowl, combine the Chinese hot oil, sesame oil, Seven-Pepper Vinegar, scallions, sugar or honey, and the salt. Heat the remaining 4 tablespoons of salad oil until almost smoking, stir, then dribble this onto the mixture in the small bowl. Let it stand and cool for 15 minutes, then pour over the noodles or spaghetti. Add the chopped parsley and toss well. Serve at room temperature.

SERVES 4 TO 10, DEPENDING ON HOW MUCH OTHER FOOD YOU'RE SERVING.

HERBAL MAYONNAISE

Homemade mayonnaise is a revelation — especially when you make it with a special flavored vinegar. This recipe calls for a food processor and takes seconds to make, but if you have nothing else to do with the rest of the day, you could beat it by hand.

    1   tablespoon Rosemary-Tarragon, Provençal, or other herb-flavored
         vinegar (see pages 10, 13, or 9)
    1   whole egg
    ¼   teaspoon prepared mustard
    1   teaspoon salt
    ¼   teaspoon white pepper
    1½   cups salad oil (or a bit less)
         Herbs to match your vinegar — 1 tablespoon fresh, minced,
            or 1 teaspoon dry

Put the vinegar, egg, mustard, salt, and pepper in the bowl of a food processor. Buzz briefly, then pour in the oil in a very thin stream. Stop adding oil when the mayonnaise is as thick as you want it to be. Stir in the herbs.

FRENCH POTATO SALAD

The French have a great approach to potato salad. Quite unlike our usual American picnic version, which is cold and laden with much mayonnaise, theirs is served warm and features vinegar, oil, and subtle seasonings.

For a classic French Potato Salad, the potatoes are peeled immediately after boiling, but many cooks now use small new potatoes, preferably red, and leave the peel on.

    2   pounds "boiling" potatoes, new or older (see above)
    ¾   cup salad oil (or, to be very French, use olive oil)
    2   tablespoons Thyme, Lemon Peel, and Black Peppercorn Vinegar
         (see page 10)
    ¼   cup minced onion or scallion
         Salt and pepper to taste
    2   tablespoons minced parsley

Boil the potatoes in salted water until just tender. Meanwhile, combine the oil, vinegar, and salt and pepper in a small saucepan. Now either peel the potatoes or don't (see above). Either way, slice them into a bowl while still hot. Bring the dressing in the saucepan just to a simmer, add the onion or scallion and parsley, and pour the mixture over the hot potato slices at once. Toss gently. The salad is ready to eat now, though its flavor will be even better if you allow it to sit for at least 30 minutes, then reheat.

SERVES 4 TO 6.

ALPINE SANDWICHES

Here's the king of all open-faced cheese sandwiches. The oil and vinegar and tarragon are very important to the flavor. I started making these because of a cheese and onion sandwich I was once served on the same plate with a green salad overflowing with tarragon dressing. It's an irresistible combination.

The roll you use must be crisp, but its size can vary. When I can find them, I like to use 6-inch "French" rolls, but even a club roll will do. Because of this size variance, I can't give you specific amounts to use, but here's what to do:

Crisp rolls (see above)
Olive oil
Tarragon vinegar
Dried tarragon, crumbled
Good Swiss cheese or Cheddar, sliced thin
Onion, cut in half and very thinly sliced

Cut the rolls in two lengthwise. Put them on a flat baking sheet. On each cut half, drizzle on some of the oil and some of the vinegar. (For a 6-inch roll, use about 2 teaspoons of each.) Now crumble some dried tarragon over this to intensify the flavor. Top with first the thinly sliced cheese, then the onion slivers. Bake at 375°F for 10 minutes or a bit more, or until the cheese has melted and the onion is beginning to change color.

AVOCADOS WITH A WARM DRESSING

This is an amazingly appealing combination. It's not just the cold avocado contrasted with the warm dressing. More than that, it's the blandness of the avocado meat with the gently spiced dressing. Fantastic!

4   tablespoons butter
¼   cup catsup
¼   cup Three-Peppercorn Vinegar (see page 11)
1   tablespoon honey
2   tablespoons meat sauce or Worcestershire
2–3 drops Hot, Hot, Hot Vinegar (see page 11)
2   avocados

Combine everything except the avocados in a small saucepan. Bring just to a boil, stirring. Cut the avocados in two lengthwise, remove the seeds, and fill the cavities with the dressing. This recipe makes more dressing than most avocado cavities can hold, but not more than most avocado lovers can eat. Put the rest in a small pitcher or bowl and pass with the avocados to be added ad lib.

SERVES 4.

RASPBERRY VINAIGRETTE

A beautiful dressing for any simple salad.

½   cup olive oil
¼   cup Raspberry Vinegar (see page 7)
2   teaspoons freshly squeezed lemon juice
Salt and freshly ground black pepper to taste

Combine all the ingredients in a screw-top jar and shake thoroughly. (Note: If you prefer a less tart dressing, you can cut the amount of vinegar down to 2 or 3 tablespoons — but do try it this way first.)

MAKES ABOUT ¾ CUP.

A nice variation: For a Blue Cheese Raspberry Vinaigrette, add ¼ cup crumbled blue cheese and mash it into the dressing.

PEASANT CAVIAR

This is also known as Eggplant Oriental (among other things), but do call it Peasant Caviar when you serve it. Even dedicated eggplant haters go wild about it. You can serve it with squares of pumpernickel or Melba toast as an appetizer or put it on a bed of lettuce for a salad.

1   eggplant (about 1 pound)
2   tablespoons olive oil
2   tablespoons Rosemary-Tarragon Vinegar (see page 10)
2   cloves garlic, finely minced or pressed
¼   cup minced onion
Salt and pepper to taste

Place the eggplant in a small pan and bake at 325°F for 2 hours or until collapsed (the eggplant, not you). When it's cool enough to handle, cut a slit in the skin and scoop out the meat. Combine with all the other ingredients. (A food processor makes this simple.) Chill.

SERVES 4 AS A SALAD OR 8 AS AN APPETIZER.

BAKED BRUSSELS SPROUTS WITH HERB VINEGAR

Give brussels sprouts a try this way, no matter how you may have felt about them in the past. They're crisp, and not strong-tasting at all.

1   pound medium-sized brussels sprouts (or larger ones, cut in half)
2   tablespoons olive oil
Salt and freshly ground black pepper to taste
1   tablespoon Basil or Tarragon Vinegar (see page 9)

Trim the root ends off, then put the brussels sprouts in a shallow baking pan. Sprinkle on the olive oil and salt and pepper, and toss to combine well. If a few of the outer leaves come off, leave them in the pan. Bake at 400°F for 15 minutes, turning once. At this point the sprouts will be bright green and just slightly crunchy. Alternately, cook for 20–25 minutes, turning twice, until the outer leaves of the sprouts are somewhat crisp. Both ways are excellent.) Just before serving, sprinkle on the vinegar and toss quickly.

SERVES 4.

TOMATOES PROVENÇAL

These are the perfect accompaniment for any main dish, except possibly one which already contains tomatoes.

2	large tomatoes
1	tablespoon Dijon mustard (optional)
¾	cup soft bread crumbs (made from homemade-type bread)
2	tablespoons minced parsley
1	tablespoon Provençal Vinegar (see page 13)
2	tablespoons olive oil

Cut the tomatoes in two across the middles. Gently squeeze out most of their seeds and the surrounding liquid, then put them upside down on paper towels to drain for 15 minutes. Now put the tomatoes halves right side up in a small, oiled baking pan. Spread the mustard on each tomato half. (This isn't exactly authentically Provençal, so omit if you wish, but it's a good touch.) Combine the bread crumbs with the parsley and put on top of the tomatoes, pressing the mixture in just a little. Sprinkle on first the vinegar, then the oil. Bake at 350°F for 20 minutes, or until the bread crumbs are crisp and brown.

SERVES 2 OR 4.

CLASSIC PICKLED EGGS

Pickled eggs were part of the now-legendary "free lunch" served if you bought a beer in bars years ago. You still see them sometimes in gallon jars on the counter in diners or country lunch places. In today's lifestyle, they have many uses. They can go on picnics, in lunchboxes, into salads or egg salad sandwiches, and they make a sensational snack at any time of the day.

6	eggs, freshly hard-boiled and peeled
1	cup onion vinegar
1	bay leaf
¼	teaspoon Hot, Hot, Hot Vinegar (see page 11)
1	half-inch piece of fresh ginger, peeled, or ¼ teaspoon ground ginger

Put the hard-boiled eggs in a screw-top jar. Combine all the other ingredients in a small saucepan and simmer for 10 minutes. While it's warm but not hot, pour the vinegar mixture over the eggs. When the vinegar is cool, cover the jar. Try to resist trying the eggs for 24 hours. As long as they're covered with the vinegar, the eggs will keep at room temperature for at least a month.

RASPBERRY-PICKLED EGGS

In addition to regular pickled eggs there are also pink ones, traditionally colored with beets. I like my pink pickled eggs to get their color — and a very special flavor — from raspberry vinegar.

6   eggs, freshly hard-boiled and peeled
1½   cups Raspberry Vinegar (see page 7)
½   cup water
1   tablespoon brown sugar
½   of a cinnamon stick
6   whole cloves

Put the hard-boiled eggs in a screw-top jar. Combine all the other ingredients in a small saucepan and simmer for 10 minutes. While it's warm but not hot, pour the vinegar mixture over the eggs. Close the top of the jar, but stir the eggs gently from time to time so they will be uniformly colored. Let them pickle for 3 days before using — if you can keep your hands off them. Keep these eggs under refrigeration.

BLUEBERRY VINEGAR CANDY

I've been making this with cider vinegar since I was a small child, and have always loved it. It's even better made with Blueberry (or Raspberry) Vinegar. Besides, you can really startle people with blue candy.

2   tablespoons butter (plus more to grease a pan)
2   cups sugar
½   cup Blueberry or Raspberry Vinegar (see pages 7–8)

Grease a large pan or cookie sheet. Melt the butter in a saucepan, then add the sugar and vinegar. Stir over medium heat until the sugar has dissolved, then turn the heat up a bit and boil gently, stirring frequently, until the mixture reaches 350°F. Pour onto the pan or cookie sheet. The candy will harden as it cools. When completely hardened, break apart into bite-sized pieces.

Alternatives: For a burnt sugar brittle, cook to 325°F. or for a vinegar taffy, cook only to 275°F, then pull.

PEACH VINEGAR PIE

Vinegar Pie goes back in American history to the time when vanilla and lemon juice were difficult to obtain, and vinegar was used as a substitute. Don't let the name "vinegar pie" scare you off. This is a fabulous dessert. You could use Raspberry or Blueberry Vinegar for this, too.

4	tablespoons butter or margarine
1	cup sugar
6	tablespoons flour
1	teaspoon mixed "pumpkin pie spice" (optional — I find this unnecessary, but many of the pioneers' added this much spice and more to their vinegar pies)
¼	cup Peach, Apricot or Nectarine Vinegar (see page 8)
2	eggs, lightly beaten
2	cups water
1	partially baked 9-inch pie shell

Cream the butter and sugar together, then stir in, in this order, the flour, spice mixture (if you're using it), vinegar, egg and water. Put into a double boiler and cook until thickened, stirring frequently. Pour into the pie shell. Bake at 350°F for 35 minutes or until set, then allow to cool before serving.